The Matriarch's Verse

Apiorkor Seyiram Ashong-Abbey

THE MATRIARCH'S VERSE

ISBN: 978 9988 8904 2 1

ABAVANNA SERIES (AV8)

Editorial Team
Dr Martin Egblewogbe

Book Layout by multiPIXEL Limited
P O Box DC 1965, Dansoman, Accra, Ghana
Email: jkojoyanney@gmail.com
Tel: +233 302 333 502 | +233 246 725 060 | +233 246 210 862

Published by
DAkpabli & Associates
P O Box 7465, Accra North, Accra, Ghana
Tel: +233 264 339 066 | +233 244 704 250 | +233 247 896 375
Email: info@dakpabli.com

ABOUT THE AUTHOR

Apiorkor Seyiram Ashong-Abbey is an award-winning Ghanaian Poet, Writer, Literary Critic, Media Practitioner, Activist and Versatile Creative of Ga-Daŋme and Ewe ancestry.

Her work is noted for its rare narrative, prosaic nature, which is uncommon, in poetry. She has also been commended for the sharp, vivid imagery of her pieces.

Living in Ghana, where oral literary traditions are intricately intertwined with deep culture and history, she performs within West Africa's most sophisticated spaces and has been featured on two TEDx platforms.

She has also been a speaker at Re:publica, the largest conference on Internet and digital society in Europe.

Her performances are varied, animated; you can expect to see Apiorkor inject life into her poems, with Classical, Afro-pop, Reggae and Rock music forms, Contemporary Dance and alternative Art. Apiorkor causes quite a stir, because the poetess chooses to read/recite her pieces on stage, rather than delivering them off memory.

She also has a West African Baobab Award, under her belt, having been awarded the "Literary and Community Building Award", which was presented to her in Lagos, Nigeria, in 2016 and which acknowledges the achievements of Africans and non-Africans in building literate communities in today's world.

When she's not creating literary orgasms, Apiorkor is most likely designing content, producing (or hosting) award-winning shows on Accra-based Citi 97.3 FM and Citi TV. As a seasoned Media Practitioner, she is also a copywriter, a voice over artist, an Events MC/ Moderator and an advertising concept designer.

Editing and proofreading documents that span a gamut of topics and structures are a strength of hers, as well.

Additionally, her work at Citi FM and Citi TV, as an activist for Literacy & Numeracy, Arts & Culture and Socio-economic development has been well received. Furthermore, Apiorkor is known for her use of New Media forms, in disseminating her Poetry and for the purposes of Activism/ Social Commentary.

As a Literature scholar, she might also be mentoring and teaching or lecturing young Ghanaians, focusing on anything from Literature, to social issues, to writing skills, to love and relationships, to career guidance. Editing and crafting pyramids of meaningful words tend to keep her occupied, as well.

Or she might be whipping up hors d'œrves for Ghanaian socialites, tasty meals for her adorable son and daughter, or romantic dinners for her husband, Frederick.

To every young person, who longs for a voice.

To every woman, who feels lost, troubled and drowned in the deep waters of societal expectations and womanhood itself.

To every disciple of the mighty pen.

To Ghana. To love. To passion. To humanity.

- A.S.A.

ACKNOWLEDGEMENTS

"True gratitude is not just a formality; it is indicative of humility, refinement, maturity and it is the attitude of those who are incessantly blessed with love, joy, peace and prosperity." – Apiorkor

There are so many people, times and spaces that I am grateful to. I shall duly acknowledge them, in no particular order.

God – My creator, my life-giver. It is You who has blessed me with the spirit of empathy and with the gift to spin bales of words, out of people's choices, experiences, successes and challenges. It is you who guides me and who has led me on this poetic journey. Thank you, for my talent. Thank you for giving me an Art, with which I can evangelise and touch lives. Thank you, for giving me the courage to highlight even the most sensitive of issues, through my pen.

My parents – Dr. Samuel Nii-Noi Ashong and Mrs. Maude Akosua Ashong. There has never been a time, when you have discouraged me from writing. You even suggest topics, for me to write on. You make it to my performances, you read and critique my work, you proudly share my gift with friends and family. You have raised me to be bold and to openly voice my opinions, without fear. You have taught me that I can be anything I want to be and do anything I want to do, regardless of what society thinks or says. Thank you for your love, support and prayers. Thank you for continually ensuring that I strive for excellence and that I do not allow the writer in me to die. I love you both.

My sisters – Mrs. Apiele Selom Lartey and Dr. Kailey Elemawusi Ashong. Your love and support have been endless. Even when people have questioned why I write, or what I write, you have defended and marketed my work, in a manner which I often could not do, myself. You are the silent watchers. The hidden foundation upon which my house is built. Thank you for being in my corner, even when it might have been difficult to do so.

My husband – Frederick "Nayo" Abbey. Freddie, where do I even begin? Many men are threatened by women who chase their dreams; but not you. From the first day I met you, you have been my biggest cheerleader. You read my poems. You give me writing prompts. You make it to my performances - you are no stranger to Ghana's Poetry scene. You sponsor my projects. You stay at home and see to our children, when I have to be out chasing dreams. You sit by me, while I keep late nights, working and writing my heart away. You have never questioned my aspirations, as a writer; you have only stood by me every step of the way, over the past 10 years, or so.

I remember how, in Uni, you used to study my poems, as though they formed portions of your course material. Then we would discuss them for hours, late into the night and I would perform some of them for you. You would hang on to my every word. You would watch me with such intensity and admiration, in your eyes. I cannot thank you enough. You will never be able to understand how your passion for what I do has impacted my life and achievements. Thank you. I love you.

My friends-turned-sisters – Ms. Sandra Fiagbedzi, Ms. Nana Ama Buckman, Mrs. Afiba Dzah, Dr. Nana Efua Wilmot, Ms. Priscilla

Akoto-Bamfo. I know that you ladies do not always understand what I do; but that has never stopped any of you from investing prayers, time and dedication in my life and work. Thank you for being there for me, for 15 years. Thank you for the beautiful and genuine sisterhood that we share.

My boss and father – Mr. Samuel Atta Mensah (Sammens). Your eye for talent is unparalleled. Your loving, yet firm disposition has been a contributing factor to this book. It is your fervent wish that I become a formidable, global force in the Literary world; and I will not disappoint you, Papa. Thank you for giving me the time, space and platform to flourish as a poet and a writer. Thank you for taking a keen interest in the development of my gift. Thank you for always telling me the truth and being a voice of reason. And thank you for all that you have done and continue to do, in ensuring that I do not rest, until I have attained my laurels. May God always bless you.

My brother and friend – Mr. Bernard Avle. Your encouragement, your belief in my abilities, your honest and timely feedback, your quest to comprehend and appreciate my work; I shall forever be grateful for all of this. Thank you for your lack of inhibition, in using your candle to light mine.

Sir Black, Chief Moomen, Rhymesonny, Nana Asaase, Hondred Percent, Crystal Tettey, Poetra, Dzyadzorm, Kwame Write, Akosua Hanson and the Writers Project of Ghana / Ghana Association of Writers/ Ehalakasa / ALEWA / P.O.E.T.S. community – You helped me to identify my voice. You gave me several stages upon which to explore myself, as an artist. How could I not be grateful for that? Thank you for respecting and promoting my Art. The love is deep.

To the sages before us – Prof. Ama Ata Aidoo, Prof. Kofi Anyidoho, Dr. Mawuli Adjei, Ayikwei Armah, Amma Darko and the many candles which together create the literary bonfire that is our heritage; thank you for writing. Thank you, for inspiring. And thank you for living in a way that has made it possible for me and for other contemporary Ghanaian writers to live too.

My brother, my creative director, my ride-or-die – Nii Quaye Aryee. Nii...we have come a long way, from those quiet afternoons at the University of Ghana, when we would simply jam and enjoy Art, for the sake of it. You kept the dream of becoming an artist alive and you dragged me along with you. Thank you, for always being there. Thank you for sharpening my craft, with your own exceptional talent. Thank you for making me laugh, when it got tough and for keeping me strong, both on the stage and off of it. Thank you for all of the sacrifices that you have made, in a bid to make me better.

To the Tema International School (TIS) community; especially to the TIS founding family and to Mrs. Surama King – You have educated me, have groomed me, have given me a chance to become a fine educator of the world and have continued to support my craft in various ways. I will forever be grateful to you all. Mrs. Comfort Adjavon, Mrs. Cecilia Ajavon-Oppan, Mrs. Frances Ajavon Okudzeto; God bless you all.

Another dear mother of mine, Mrs. Helena Kpatakpa – Your love, your counsel and your prayers will always be with me. You are a true blessing and even though I might not always say so, please never doubt it. Thank you, for everything.

To Ms. Frema Adunyame – Thank you for believing in my craft and for the time and dedication, which you have invested in "brand Apiorkor". I cannot thank you enough.

To Ms. Magdalene Williams – My clothes, my makeup, my emotional well-being; you have made sure that it is all in stellar condition. Very few people would spend sleepless nights to make another person look good and all for no fee! Sis, the love is deep. Thank you.

Mr. J.B. Allotey – My brother, you have been a pillar in my life. Thank you for the prayers, advice, guidance, the pep talks and for sharing your beautiful mind with me.

Mr. Nii Darku Otoo (A.K.A. MoShutter) – My "son"; through your camera lens and through your eyes, I have often seen and experienced a better version of myself. Not only have you captured and documented some of the most intimate and memorable aspects of my life, but you have also become a crucial part of my life, ever present to remind me of my brilliance. Thank you.

Mr. Bernard Arthur – You are a brother and a friend. Enough said. I appreciate you so much.

Mr. Kojo Akoto Boateng – Thank you for always being in my corner and for sharing my visions with me.

To Dr. Helen Wireko and Dr. Cameron Anto-Boateng – My sister and brother from another mother; you have been in my lives, forever. Thank you for sticking around long enough, to see the woman that I have become.

Dr. Bernard Akoi-Jackson, Mr. Courage Nobi, Stephen Kofi Dotse, Ms. Emefa Tsikata – My crazy, creative, patriotic tribe. Thank you for pushing me along, on this journey.

Prof. Atukwei Okai, Mr. Alphonse Ajavon, Mr. Noel Mensah Kpatakpa, Mr. Keli Tsikata – All of blessed memory. May the you all continue to rest in perfect peace, even as I pay homage to you, for the massive impact and influence, which each of you has had on my life and on my Art. You shall never be forgotten.

Dearest Auntie Abla Dzifa Gomashie, big sister Juliet Asante – I cannot overlook the lengths to which both of you have gone, just to make sure that I would never even think of neglecting my craft and my dreams. There is so much that many women can learn from you, particularly when it comes to empowering other women to simply be… This is for you, ladies.

To my Citi FM / Citi TV family and particularly to Ms. Jessica Opare Saforo, Ms. Sandister Tei, Mrs. Jennifer Anane-Nsiah, Mrs. Vivian Kai Lokko, Ms. Ogboe Adusu – Thank you for your daily doses of encouragement. Thank you for recognising my gifts. Thank you for working tirelessly to maintain an environment that is conducive for crazy creatives and dreamers, like me.

To Arc. Felix Abbey & Mrs. Sarah Abbey – Daddy and Mummy, I am ever grateful for the fact that you have taken me as your daughter. I am blessed to have parents-in-law like you and I thank you for continually celebrating my achievements.

To the late Madam Cecilia Praeger Abbey – To have met you, would have been a great honour; but the Lord always has his own map drawn out for us. Nonetheless, your son has brought so much love, joy and prosperity into my life. Thank you for bringing him into this world and for shielding us with your prayers, even as you rest in perfect peace.

To Delasi Akyea-Djamson, Yiela Akyea-Djamson, Edinam Annan-Wuaku, Elikem Annan-Wuaku and Eyram Annan-Wuaku – Thank you for loving and cheering me on, family. I love you all.

To my sons Iain Lartey and Ivan Lartey, whom I love so much – Always know and remember that you motivate me to be better.

To Mr. Duke Lartey Jnr. And Mr. Danny Quaye – Brothers-in-law turned brothers. Your love and encouragement shall never be forgotten. Much love to you, both.

DAkpabli & Associates, Dr. Martin Egblewogbe – You have brought my Art to life and have etched it into the stones of centuries to come. How can I thank you for that? Thank you for believing in me and in what I have to say to the world.

To Angela Darke, DJ JayJay, Pearl Hammond, Emmanuel Olele Sarpong, Jeffrey Owuraku Sarpong, Priscilla Buaba-Lemdy, Mercy Adjorlolo – And to all of the other young women and men, who inspire me on a daily basis. It is because of you that I have the strength to create and to be better. Please never stop demanding more of me and please continue to give me space in your daily lives and within your hearts, as I humbly work to do my best for young Ghanaians and for this nation which has birthed us.

My precious children; my son Frederick Matey Donolo Abbey Jnr and my daughter Melina Nakoyo Abbey – You two have brought me so many blessings. You have redefined love, in my eyes. Even as I labored to carry and to birth you both, you gave me strength from within and led me to achieve wonderful things and to attain admirable laurels. My children, may God bless you, beyond your wildest imaginations. May He always position me to bring nothing but favour, honour and pride to you and to the Abbey / Ashong-Abbey name. I love you both, so much.

To The United States of America – Land of my birth. The place which served as home to me, during my formative years and during young adulthood. The country, which has marked my heritage and mind, so indelibly. God bless America.

Finally, to every heartbreaker, to people who stabbed me in the back, to the evil plotters and doers, to the ones who brought me euphoria and to them who doused me in seemingly endless pain…to anyone who ever doubted my capabilities, to all those who ever spoke ill of me, to the strangers, lovers, friends, people and things – I praise God, for enabling me to turn my pain, joy, successes and failures into something so grand.

Love, Joy and Peace abound to all!

FOREWORD

Apiorkor Ashong-Abbey represents a new crop of eclectic artists, whose skill in various art forms enables her to reach a wide array of audiences on stage, via media and through the written word.

Her writings combine the quality of some of Ghana's greats, such as Atukwei Okai, Kofi Anyidoho and Ama Ata Aidoo, with the simplicity to reach today's tech-savvy generation of Art consumers.

The Matriarch's Verse is a skillfully woven cover-cloth of many colours, comprising strands of history, philosophy, faith, hope and love.

Enigmatic, yet thoroughly engaging, this work is in the form of poetic potions that one can consume daily, to stimulate the mind and to soothe the soul.

You will meet interesting portraits of periods, places and people.

And, in the daily capsules, you will not only experience Apiorkor the Poet, but also get the privilege to meet Apiorkor the person: gifted composer, breathtaking performer, passionate lover and amazing Mother.

Bernard Avle
General Manager, Citi FM/Citi TV and Host of the Award-winning Citi Breakfast Show

CONTENTS

WHEN WORDS WIN YOU OVER

For those of us who have become disciples of writing, being able to put strokes of ink upon paper is a rare gift. A gift that affords us the opportunity to escape into a world so different from the one that we wake up to each morning, by God's gracious making. A gift that enables us to express ourselves in a medium void of judgment and ridicule. A gift that, really and truly, permits us to explore our inner identity, whilst we gather the courage and confidence to share the core of our very being with others...

As a young girl, I had always longed to be a great writer. I wanted to be able to write a piece in ten minutes tops. I wished that I would be able to exercise enough discipline, that I could chronicle my thoughts and emotions. I needed to be a part of that awesome literary world. I resolved that, with time, I would possess enough strength to impart knowledge, to convey powerful messages to world, via the potency of the word.

And not only did I sit and daydream of these things. I read books, journals, letters, my Bible, I read and still do read my dictionary, committing to memory five to ten words daily. Above all, I practised. Just as a well acclaimed musician works at her violin, or as a jockey, constantly, rides his horse hard, I went all out, where my writing was concerned. I would create short stories and then ask my parents to read them over. I wrote poetry, made scripts of drama pieces. All I ever wanted to do was be an artist; I wanted to paint pictures, but with words.

I can vividly recall the day that I became absolutely, downright smitten with words. I was five months into my fourteenth year, my older cousin took my sisters, other cousins and I to one of Ghana's beaches. As usual, I was in awe, when I took in the setting. The breeze caught the scarf on my head, the salty waters glistened, as though tiny gems had been dispersed upon the big sea's surface. I threw off my sandals, walked to a spot on the sand, about 15 ft away from everyone else. I sat, not even bothering to lay out my blanket first. I pulled out a homework book from my canvas bag, then a pencil (I always preferred to do my math in pencil). I began my work, moving at a steady pace…

I have always loved the beach- the soft, yet coarse, damp sand tickling my feet; the vast oceans in their seemingly endless entirety; the subtle, often harsh sea breeze upon my face; and oh, the lighting! Be it a sun kissed beach, or a moonlit one- even at a tender age, the beach always put me in the best of moods. And I would soon come to a realisation that those very sands and waters shall be my inspiration to write any piece at all. They would be the single, collaborating cure for my writer's block, any day, any time.

As I write, I am still unsure of what came over me at that moment on the beach, on that September morning. All I can remember is watching my math book close. My little 'writing diary', as I had called it, lay on my lap now, my pencil remained in my hand. And I wrote ten poems at a go! If I felt tired, or lazy, all I had to do was look out, towards the ocean before me- and then I was re-energised at once!

The feeling was inexplicable. I lost track of everything around me, save my book and my pencil. Suddenly, I understood myself better and I was ready to depict me, to share my thoughts, perceptions, opinions and emotions with other people. I felt liberated. I had discovered a new medium of expression...

This is what happens, when words win you over. You do not become a slave to words, no. On the contrary, you gain possession of the power that equips you with the required skill, that you can now arrange and rearrange words. You can tailor a group of words to suit the context, in which you wish to speak. You have command over the Language. All of this is really as a result of one bold, courageous step. Yes, it does take courage to write. When you are immersed in what you are writing, you no longer have control over what you are communicating to your readers, because your emotions, ideas and all those other things that you are putting into manuscript, they wash over you and breathe life into the vocabulary, into the diction, into the words. For that matter, your soul is bared for all to see. Now tell me I am wrong in saying that, one needs to be extremely courageous, in order to allow this to happen.

Hence, we can say that, when words win you over, your psyche-your state of mind- is greatly affected, because your conscious mind gives way to the sub conscious and this is why we say that writing takes you into another realm, where self-expression means pouring your heart out incessantly. This is especially true of poetic writing.

In short, writing is like love: it is hard for anyone to decipher the chemistry that exists between people, who love each other. One remains a stranger to love and love a stranger to one, until the one in question discovers love with another. You can only truly solve the mystery of writing, when you begin to speak the language of a writer: And that, my friends, will be the very point at which words will win you over.

2007

The Human Experience

SOME KIND OF WATER THERAPY

Water. The Ocean. Sunset.
Whenever this Ga girl is pensive,
Whenever this daughter of Earth has a mind tormented with incoherence,
The waves obey the heatwaves of her blazing mind...

Inspiration. Motivation. Tranquility.

I went home and all became well again.
The ebb and flow of those powerful waves that mirror the undiluted strength of my God... that moving water which is infused with the age-old blood of Christ... that gushing water healed my bruised soul.
Water. The Ocean. Sunset.
My single, twisted cure.

2016

LOVE

I encase myself within the bosom of Love.
Love is who I'd like to marry, to live with, to birth.
Love is who I want to be.

2015

CHOICES I

I choose to see beauty in the passion of hatred, as opposed to seeing hatred, itself...

2015

CHOICES II

Sometimes the sound of my own laughter spurs me on.
I tell myself that if I've laughed once, I can do it again.
I shouldn't be the cold ashes of the inferno of my passion. I must
blaze till the day I die...

2015

I MET LOVE

You can't know love, until you meet her, touch her, hear her, love her… you can't know love until you know her.

27

2015

PURE, UNADULTERATED LOVE

You will never be able to comprehend the hold you have on my heart.
You recognised my potential, even from the very start.
Your eyes mirror my dreams, my nightmares; they pour tears for my failures and they shine with mist for my victories.
Your intelligence fascinates me and the sway of your hips captivates me. I love you…

You will never comprehend how strongly my heart beats for you.
You value my intellect and it does not intimidate you.
Forget makeup and handbags and stilettos and diamonds and gold; you are my most valuable possession, my priceless accessory.
When I shiver in sickness, your teardrops and the feathery touch of your masculine fingers are my healing salve. I love you…

Our love has very little to do with late night aphrodisiacs and hard, aggressive thrusts and howling screams
That echo shallow climaxes, which can easily be replicated by another sex-rod, or another sex-pot, which have been coupled with high libido and more late-night aphrodisiacs.
Our love has never been about exquisite gifts, diamonds and bigger gems, cars and mansions, or socialite dinners,
Which will be forgotten at 1.00 am, when they cannot heat up the icy, pricey, ruby-red satin and silk sheets on the other side of the bed.
Our love doesn't hide beneath the cloak of delicate flowers and frilly, fancy cards and crisp, polished words, which do not really say what we mean, when we mean it.

And our love doesn't know harsh, verbal weapons that stab at our hearts, suffocate our emotions and cut into wounds that have long shed their scabs,
And our love is ignorant of cold, iron fists that burn red-hot with a raging anger that is birthed by hate,
Our love lives in a realm where the only two mortal spirits are you and I, just making a lengthy, unique journey together,
And we lose our way:
We starve a little, when we're low on love-food and our throats are parched, when the refreshing love-waters morph into saline Dead-Sea-Waters.
We trip over our feet a little, when our love is gasping for air, because we're strangling it with frustration and unkindness...

But this love does continue to survive, because she recognised his potential, even from the very start.
And her eyes mirror his dreams, his nightmares; they pour tears for his failures and they shine with mist for his victories.
And her intelligence fascinates him and the sway of her hips captivates him and he yearns for her smooth, fleshy thighs to intertwine with his taut, muscular pelvis.

Yes, this love does continue to survive, because he values her intellect and it does not intimidate him.
And forget makeup and handbags and stilettos and diamonds and gold; he is her most valuable possession, her priceless accessory.
And when she shivers in sickness, his teardrops and the feathery touch of his masculine fingers are her healing salve, and she day-dreams of his chisel-carved chest engulfing her delicately scented lady-mounds...

This love is not a perfect love and can never be... But it is a pure, unadulterated love.

2015

A VALEDICTION... TO A LIFE OF BEAUTY

We often take smiles, aces and conversations for granted.
We eat, drink, dance, gossip; eat, drink, dance and gossip some more...

Your smile was, indeed, beautiful.

All you had to do was to part your lips and then everything was all right.
Those teeth had a way of shining beams straight into lives, into hearts, into spirits and into souls; like the vile cancer that transformed your body.

And then, of course, that smile had its way of Hypnotising the ladies...

Your face WAS handsome.
No woman with blood running through her veins and swaying hips could walk by you without doing a double take.
And your heart was handsome; you lived by the motto of generosity, you loved hard, until we could see the love pour out of your eyes in dollops of glee and grief.

Your words were more than hearty.
It was hard to zip our lips, when we were with you, because you'd talk and laugh and joke and tickle and prod, until words would gush out of our mouths, like water bursting out of a broken pipe by the roadside.

And talking to you was easy because, we could see our pain in your fists, our joy on your lips, our sorrow in the crease of your forehead, our turbulent, unstable emotions in the centres of your eyes; you didn't judge.

But we took that beautiful smile for granted.
We overlooked that handsome face.
We quickly forgot those hearty conversations...

And today, we cannot eat, drink, dance and gossip and as we scream heavy verses, we're not even sure if you can hear us or not. And if you can, know that your life was one of beauty, one to be celebrated, one to be written about in the books of the living.

2015

THE LONER

The clouds are monstrous...
Sun hides her beautiful, glittering face from Earth.
Time crawls heavily on its belly, slithering along in pain, agony and dejection.

I have not seen Moon for ages...
Her tranquil, romantic glow is only a gloomy shadow;
And the clouds are monstrous, as they push and shove her.
The ruthless clouds bruise her, strip her of her bright beauty, within and without.

The sweet aroma of Mother Nature's delicate girl-petals evades me...
They have lost their youthful shine,
They have been robbed of their balmy softness.
And the clouds are monstrous, as they persuade Wind to cast an icy spell upon these fragile ladies.

Sleep would be the best painkiller, but she will not come.
The brow is drenched and the entire being burns, as though set to smoulder on a spit.
Yet the blood is cold and her lips are blue with sorrow.
The clouds have been terribly monstrous.

They have spat in the face and commanded Wind to blow the disgusting liquid dry.
And together with the spittle, the once boiling blood turns a sticky mass.

Where is the heartbeat, where is it?
Slowly, the body deteriorates and the spirit dies, while the soul sublimes...

And does no one see it all?
Does one live in a bubble, so that one's anguish cannot be seen, the tears tasted, the wailing heard?
Can a person be so invisible? So easily ignored? Left to suffer alone?
Or is it one's sheer un-importance, one's excessive deconstruction in another's mind?
Do people not value other people, their own people, as was once the norm?

Then: NOTHING! Nothing...
Void of feeling.
Seeing no more.
And all is lost now...
For an emotional, spiritual death supersedes a mere perishing of the flesh.
It remains Eternal.

2012

WHEN I BREATHE NO MORE...

The sun's eyes will tear up and splatter gold nuggets all over the Universe...
The lesser stars will converge in a huge circle and dance a most sprite-ly dance, their unparalleled flexibility causing sparks and shine to fly about in wild abandon...
The waters will rise from their stony beds and reign, torrential-ly, over people, animals and houses, like the spittle of a trotro driver,
At the crack of dawn on Friday-mourning...
The wind will scream in key G and the grass will strum a dirge...

When I die...
Men and women will rejoice with hollow hymns and rusty cymbals and bottles of this and that and malt...
Other men will lament at never having banged-it-up against a wall, never having to worry about hearts, love and attachments-unwanted-unsolicited, as they walk with satiated pelvic regions...
Other women might follow the suit of the other men, but many of the other women will reminisce about high heels, long hair, soft hair, makeup and too-known-ness...
Children with snotty noses will blow a booger or two into mummy's handkerchief and infants will suck and suck and suck nipples dry, until they collapse into drunken sleep; then other children and infants will cry for an aunty...

When I die...
Time. Will. Stop.
The ringing in my ears will become deafening;
The burning in my eyes will sting and attempt to wrench these balls out of their homely sockets;

The tingling on my skin will escalate into a torturous peeling of my skin;

The itching of my tongue will weaken it, so that it so much as touches my teeth and then in an instant, hangs only by a single mucous-y, saliva-ful fibre;

The blockage in my nose will intensify till air becomes but an army of irritating, painful, prickly thorns...

Then I breathe no more...

And when I breathe no more, when I die, I will be remembered a little, forgotten a lot, then remembered a little, once again; until it's time for life to trudge on.

But God and Mother Nature will mourn a child of Friday, a woman of faith:

When I die... When I breathe no more...

2014

ODE TO A TURBULENT MIND

Morning broke and Sun shone her brilliant and captivating smile upon us...
The birds painted pictures in the skies with their feather-light wings
The morning mosquitoes laid their eggs in the waters of the village water-pots.
The petal-daughters of Nature's womb blushed at the caress of the dew-kiss and the vultures sword-slashed carcasses-of-past-glory.
The mothers of the jungles pawed along, clawing at the backs and throats of their prey...

And we remained ignorant of Death's brutal plan to claw at your back, your throat; you were his prey and we were oblivious to your impending role-play as another victim in the horror-ible PLOT of the drama of Life and Death...
So Sun shone, birds air-painted, mosquitoes laid, petals bloomed and blushed, vultures sword-slashed, jungle mothers clawed:
And then we awoke, wide-eyed and drowsy-looking like innocent, naive babies with the frothy spittle of blanketing sleep, at the corners of our heavy, sticky mouths...
And you were gasping for the precious, gracious, merciful breath of-life.
And we did not know, no, we did not know...
Because we know what-was, what-is, but not what-will-be:
And we did not know that what-would-be would be a world with raw, festering, calcium-starved sores that will not clot; so blood oozes, gushes and flows with the inextinguishable fire of pain that consumes our insides;

An anger so passionate and unhealthy... And yet somehow we can make peace, because we know that you departed with the stamp of peace upon your heart...

For turbulent as your life had been, somehow you swam in a perfect cadence, at one with the ebb and flow of a filth-cleansing ocean.

The world was your home;

- AFRICA sculpted the foundation of your burdened heritage;

- The United States of America birthed you;

- Egypt was a love cocoon who gazed upon your flesh-consuming kind of love - then Egypt watched you, a wounded, bruised butterfly, your wings saturated with the putrid stench of a love gone rancid;

- Ghana stood firm, as the rugged, zealous and tortured fires of the black race consumed you

- You were a Wordsmith sculptures of word-molecules worshipped you and yielded to the torture of your hands. And from these you crafted monuments of universal truths and your literary prowess came alive with the potency of a well-endowed man-sac.

- You wore the prides, the joys, the sorrows and the shames spaces and of people, who you never knew, but who dreamt of you, people who wanted to be like you, people who cherished you; people who mourn you, now...

Now... Now... The flesh of your body is at the mercy of flesh-devouring pests.

But thoughts of you are engraved upon our brains.

Your legacy will live on. Your story will be told, you Phenomenal Woman.

And even in death, you still rise to places that, in life, many can only dream of...

And even after Sun shines no more, when birds air-paint only in historical Science books, when mosquitoes lay eggs only in memory and theory, when petals droop with icy countenance, when vultures are but fossils, as jungle mothers limp in deathly shadows:

Your immortality shall prevail on Earth, in galaxies, in unknown realms, in the face of turbulence and in another life!

2014

KEEPING LOVE ALIVE

At some point the love will dwindle.

At some point the love will elude you.

At some point you will question your choice.

At some point you will want to take back your decision.

At some point her food will taste tasteless.

At some point you will blame her and her womb for your financial troubles.

At some point you will resent your mother for asking for grandchildren.

At some point you will coil up on your luxurious couch, on a Saturday morning with cold feet and a glass of the world's finest wine, wondering where he slept last night and did what with whom.

At some point her derrière will be less like a juicy, red apple and more like an oblong loaf of bread.

At some point his belly will jiggle like the massive bowls of punch at the parties which you enjoyed going to, in your early 20's.

At some point the kisses will be laced with a bitter after-taste.

At some point the passionate love-making will morph into boring, mundane, dutiful sex.

At some point his man-stick will not fill you up like it used to.

At some point her hair will smell musty, old and dry; much unlike the fresh sea breeze that used to caress it in the Sunday Sunset at the Labadi Beach.

At some point his cologne will slap you in the face like the smell of death in a morgue.

And that's okay; that's normal.

It's life.

It's human nature.

It's the human being's insatiable appetite for BETTER things, for NEWER things, for MORE.

It's MARRIAGE.

But:

Continue to eat together.

Continue to rub her swollen feet.

Continue to bath together.

Continue to cook for him, as though you were the world's most renowned chef.

Continue to love even when there's no more love to give, even when your soul is aching with questions about what could have, would have and should have been.

At some point the love will dwindle.

At some point the love will elude you.

At some point you will question your choice.

At some point you will want to take back your decision.

And that's okay. That's alright.

But NEVER cease to Keep the LOVE alive.

2017

THE PROMISE

You never promised this road would be easy:

You never promised there wouldn't be heartache.
You never promised this life would be void of pain.
You never promised tears wouldn't gush out of my soul and dry me up, so that I become a desert.
You never promised a utopia, where we'd be drowning in milk and honey, swimming through oceans of content.
You never promised that there wouldn't be sleepless nights, which look on, as I writhe in unquenchable agony that devours my flesh and my insides.
You never promised the fidelity of a saint.
You never promised that there wouldn't be men enticing me with their words of sweet-poison or woman caressing him with their murderous tongues, lies and fingertips.
Dear God,
You never promised this road would be easy...
But You did promise that this union would be
Worth the hurt,
Worth the pain,
Worth the trials and tribulations,
Worth the tears,
Worth the struggle to keep a marriage afloat and a-kindle!
Worth Every Smile,
Worth Every Butterfly in the stomach,
Worth Every Electrifying moment of intimate satisfaction,
Worth Every Conversation at the crack of dawn,

Worth every chance to watch you sleep at night.
Worth every moment that emotion drips from your tongue, from
your eyes, as you tell me that you love me,
Worth every child of my womb,
Worth every spark in your eye, when I remind you that we've come
a long way.
Worth every prayer we've ever prayed together as man and wife,
And
Worth every battle we've fought side by side and won!

Father above,
You never promised this road would be easy...
But you did promise You would travel the distance with us and
make this marriage a Ministry.

And because we believe in Your promise,
Because You have never failed us,
We will not smile every day, no,
We will LAUGH in unison, because this Ministry is our calling and
we'll use it to glorify and to proclaim the miracle that is
Your beautiful institution of marriage.

2018

ABOUT HEARTS & HURTS

There are times when I wish that my heart knew how to hate, but it doesn't:
It's pure, it's ripe with Godly goodness and it beats with a humble-pride.
To trample on my good heart is akin to battering the heart of God, for the blood that it pumps is pigmented with the potency of His spirit...
And when I recall this, I fall in love with my heart all over again and I worship Him, who placed it within me.

2018

NOTE TO SELF

Think, Learn, Grow... every single day of your life.

You can never know too much, because you can never know everything.

And we often think that we know things, when we truly don't, anyway.

Learn from everyone and everything around you, because no one person or thing has a monopoly of knowledge.

Never be ashamed to seek answers and never fear to be proven wrong.

You should only be afraid and embarrassed to display your ignorance on a daily basis.

2017

OF VOWS & LOVE

I promise to forever sing praises with you.
I promise that I'll always worship the Creator, by your side.
I promise that I'll be your most pressing and constant reminder to thank Him; through my presence and my deeds...
Our union is divine; I've never had any doubts about that.
So it is only right that we continually and incessantly thank, praise and worship our Maker for making us a real and physical manifestation of LOVE –
Of LOVE unconditional and of LOVE divine.

2017

THE ARTIST'S CREED

Serenity graces intellectual chaos... I remember when being intellectual was chaotic and that kind of chaos could choke you.

Then we got to the point where intellect was sexy, attractive, provocative, showy; it was flex to be an intellectual.

In the later years, intellect became a true asset, a necessity that could either propel you to a pedestal or throw you into a remote galaxy, cutting you off from the air supply of your deep cultural roots... Then you were choking again.

But some of us still breathe, even beneath the ocean of intellect.

We adapt like aquatic creatures, because our Art gives us the fins and gills to bask in our vast wet and chaotic home... Intellect can't choke us.

Intellect nourishes us and becomes the sanity for our artistic chaos!

So although I'm worn and bruised and my spine aches from sitting behind a desk and my brain is shutting down, because I've been trying to sound intellectual all day:

Serenity graces intellectual chaos...

And I will bask within the tranquility of my Art that balances out that intellectual insanity.

2016

EASY SUNDAYS OF TURBULENCE

Cocooned within a shell of stress, neck ache and a love that cures the kink in my back...

Palms and palm trees that choke my brain, until it is breathless enough to cough out dark and soulful words...

Maybe I like it this way and maybe I'd rather be an infant, at liberty to wade in and out of sleep, pausing my motions, only to suckle a nipple for the hundredth time...

But this is my life.

Easy Sundays of turbulence roll quickly into Draining Mondays of chaos...

Looking forward to those random dawns of passionate love that make it all better.

2016

BEAUTIFUL MOURNING

Tall, white candles, alight in a twisted celebration of life.

Soft, melodious voices, in edification of beauty in an ugly situation.

Words of praise, drenched in saline tears of angry, sorrowful blood.

Sweet, petalled fragrances jetting far and wide in a fine mist that rests on my skin, my neck, my cheeks, my cleavage;

It's almost as though the sweet beauty of death horrifying is bathing me, embalming me, encapsulating me in a moist trance...

Last week Fiifi's brother, Ekow, called me at 1.47 am.

Mara was missing, he said.

She had run off to a meeting two mornings ago, planting a cold, breathy kiss on his lips, and he had framed her hips with his fingertips, as she spun around to fly through the front door.

My. Heart. Froze.

I panicked. I screamed. Fiifi woke up...

On Saturday, I zombied my way through the airport. South Africa was bleak. She didn't envelope me in a warm, welcoming embrace, the way that I was accustomed to.

She gazed at me through guerrilla glass. She froze the guerrilla glass; I couldn't see her eyes to bore my eyes through her eyes; right, deep, into her icy soul – in vengeance for Mara...

I collapsed into Ekow's chest. South Africa had frozen my legs.

I couldn't think. South Africa had frozen my mind...

Mara's smile caressed my eyes, as I finally began to look around the room.

She was beautiful.

Even when we were five, and we used to smear our lips and chins with chocolate and palm nut soup; even then, Mara was beautiful...

Our mothers used to drape us in twin butter-cream and pink dresses, complete with black jelly shoes to match.

Even then, she was beautiful.

Mara was a year older than I was and when, at 12, my breasts were swollen with adolescence, she at 13, was still carrying the buds of nipples that the Maker had plastered onto her chest.

But you see, Mara's beauty shone through even then;

She still wore her butter-cream and pink twin dress with class and an infantile, girlish elegance.

And she never stopped talking about how lovely I was,

How beautifully I had blossomed,

She was elated about my adolescent achievements...

And today, even in death-hideous-frozen,

My friend is beautiful.

Even with the ugly, grotesque scars that dark-brown-black-skinned brothers and sisters have etched into her cheeks and torso,

She is beautiful.

The undertaker had long scrubbed away the scarlet blood-tears that hatred, ignorance and cruelty had tattooed Mara's body with.

But the shadows of the thick, scarlet blood-tears remain, stretching and piercing through my chest, wrenching at my heart;

Even so, she is beautiful.

Even as the Ghanaian fraternity in this port city of Durban mobilises itself to trudge on home to safety, to a shelter away from this icy torture,

Mara lays with mutilated limbs.

But:

Tall, white candles, alight in a twisted celebration of life.

Soft, melodious voices, in edification of the beauty in an ugly situation.

Words of praise, drenched in saline tears of angry, sorrowful blood.

Sweet, petalled fragrances jetting far and wide in a fine mist that rests on my skin, my neck, my cheeks, my cleavage;

It's almost as though the sweet beauty of death horrifying is bathing me, embalming me, encapsulating me in a moist trance...

And I mourn my beautiful friend, having lost her to the frozen, still-born ugliness that South Africa's womb has birthed.

2015

STRUGGLING DAILY

Some days pale in comparison to others.
Some days are colour-rich, bursting with pinks and
reds and blues and yellows and green... and. black.
Some days come wrapped in blankets that have been
washed in tears so deep, that they've been blood-coloured.
Some days are full of youthful energy, blazing with the
fireballs of Earth's famous Sun, shining star Pegasus
and the glamorous Big Dipper.
Some days my jaw is locked in a perpetual maze of
confusing confusion.
Some days, my teeth and my face fall in love again,
just long enough to make passionate love, to conceive
a ghost-smile that mimics a wholesome joy that once
was, which once lived.
Some days pale in comparison to others.
They really and truly do.
But all I ask is that I might once again live some better
Days with you.

2018

DREAM WEDDING

Clinking, tinkling glasses.

Aromatic whiffs of fragrances, so delicious, that with every breath, you're drawn closer to a welcome drunkenness.

Soft, graceful butter-yellow whispers of light, bouncing off of creams, pinks, golds, a scarlet, a sky here and there.

A beam of teeth. A bridge of teeth.

Teeth peeping through Botox.

A narrow, winding, chocolate path of leg… A smooth, fleshy 15 inches of thigh. A quaintly-satin-ed leg-thigh.

Spring faces, Autumn faces.

Endless braids, tiny braids, buns, wraps, Brazilian, Peruvian, Indian tresses. Kinky-coily masses.

A "smiiiiiiiiiiiile!"…A "cheeeeeeeese!"… A zoom, A flash.

She began to glide in between the stark white chairs, with their lacey-gold attire, oblivious to the blaring music.

She was beautiful.

Somehow her presence captivated you, rising above

The crystal, the fragrances, the colour-spectrum of gowns and bow-ties and cravats, the grins full of secrets,

The 40-year-old Miss who had vowed to find a soul-mate that night with her thigh,

The gentleman who was aching to be husband-not-friend-zoned…

She glowed as she floated to Fiifi's side, her hue bouncing off of the crystal in her hand, the stone on the finger.

And he was bewitched by her. His eyes, hands, lips, were on her hair, cheeks, hands;

Love was oozing from his pores and it was obvious that their honeymoon wouldn't be one of the Harmattan.

Amina was short of breath, drowning in his ocean of affection and admiration.

And as they shared sacred whispers, dainty kisses and secrets-made-new by their new-joy,

They remained oblivious to the tens-of-thousands of Ghana Cedis that had been expertly laid out about them, for them, in celebration of their union…

Then the closing prayer was said in their honour.

But they couldn't hear it.

They didn't need it.

Surely, God could never forsake two people, who missed a prayer because their hearts were beating so loudly, so vibrantly that the prayer-sayer's voice became mute;

Could He?

2014

DEATH CAN LIVE

My heart is broken.
My heart is bruised.
My heart is battered.
My heart has been ground into a paste of bloody pain.
My heart has been shattered into one million odd and bloody pieces.

Stop.
Breathe.
Look up.
Look. At. Me.
My chest is smothered in red chunks of the fluid that is supposed to flow through my veins.
Thick, viscous drops of blood spill across this floor, as I walk, as I run, as I jump, as I try to reach You, up there!

Stop.
Breathe.
Look up.
Look. At. Me.
My eyes are red with agony, as crimson bubbles force their way into my head, into my eye sockets.
I'm drowning in this deep, dark red, nasty, smelly, bloody pool...
My heart is broken.
My heart is bruised.
My heart is battered.
My heart has been ground into a paste of bloody pain.
My heart has been shattered into one million odd and bloody pieces.

Stop.
Breathe.
Look up.
Look. At. Me.
I'm a mess, I'm dead inside, I'm a ghost of myself,
I'm wretched, useless, hopeless and disgusting.
But dear Lord God;
Precious Father...
Bulwark
Who has won impossible battles,
Who has slain gladiators,
Who has fed thousands with nothing,
Who has healed the sick,
Who has raised the DEAD,

You Who created me... My Lord God I beg You to just
Stop.
Breathe.
Look up.
Look. At. Me.
Breathe. On. Me.
Kiss. Me.
Lay. Your. Potent. Hands. On. Me.
Speak. To. Me.
Hold. Me.
Wash me clean of my gory, filthy blood stains, with your purifying
blood... Heal me, for I am terminally ill.
Resurrect me, for I am dead inside!
Breathe life into my soul again, dear God;
Save me now!
My heart is broken.

My heart is bruised.
My heart is battered.
My heart has been ground into a paste of bloody pain.
My heart has been shattered into one million odd and bloody
pieces.

Stop.
Breathe.
Look up.
Look. At. Me.
My chest is smothered in red chunks of the fluid that is supposed
to flow through my veins.
Thick, viscous drops of blood spill across this floor, as I walk, as I
run, as I jump, as I try to reach You, up there!

But Dear God, Precious Father, Strong Deliverer, Death Defeater;
I am Yours!
Act now, that my soul may live once again!

2018

WINDOWS

Windows are not always made of gleaming, tempered glass.

Windows can't always be stained with carefully mixed red, blue and golden-brown dyes.

Sometimes windows are tinted with the blood that a mangled heart shed last year....

But you wouldn't see it that way; you can only see the artistically plastered scars if the present, the hope of the now, the rejuvenation of today...

Other times windows are gaping holes that are framed by raw wood and heavy air:
And the stench of fresh air can be nauseating, when you're used to having oxygen choke you, spit on you, swallow you and then leave you to writhe in agony...

But then again,
Windows are not always made of shiny, tempered glass.

And

Windows can't always be stained with carefully mixed red, blue and golden-brown dyes.

Once you can accept this, once you can rise to the surface of the waters that drown you,

Only then can you see the window...
And then although the first gasps of air sting your lungs, you will live and birth life again.

2019

HUSTLER'S PARADISE

Dear Your Excellency John Dramani Mahama,

Allow me to begin by saying that I do respect and admire you, immensely.

Unlike many Ghanaians, I believe that our president; regardless of our individual political affiliations and sentiments; deserves our respect. After all, being the Head of State of a nation could not possibly be a walk in the park.

Having said this, though, you must not take it to necessarily mean that I identify with and glorify the political ideologies and practices that characterise and depict the political colours of your divide.

Additionally, quite frankly, none of your known political contenders has proven to me that his or her camp would make a SIGNIFICANTLY better alternative for the Ghana that I love so deeply.

However, lately, Ghana has become a HUSTLER'S PARADISE. The trouble with this is that, albeit I am an ambitious Ghanaian woman of creative dissidence, the fact remains that I was not born to HUSTLE.

Therefore, I am an unhappy Ghanaian, at the moment. My ambition is bathed in filthy, gooey, smelly, revolting, mucous-y spittle.

My creativity is stunted, because I am forced to give so much of the maximum, just so that I can attain the bare minimum. The foundation of my dissidence is shaken. I have lost my way. I am losing myself. My days are full of a blazing sun that feeds off of the migraine that has become the plague of my brain. My spirit is broken and I kneel, I pray, I hope, I speak prosperity into my life, and into the seemingly infertile womb of Ghana.

I have tried to channel my ambition, creativity and dissidence into a single, massive ball of an adrenaline-charged HUSTLE!

But, Your Excellency, I was not born to HUSTLE.

Seeing as I believe in giving people the chance to prove themselves to be different from what public and mass perceptions and conceptions might convey,

I would be most grateful, Your Excellency, if you would let me know how you can help to (in the least) mitigate the effects of this predicament, within which I find myself.

And why do I ask you, you say?

Why have I not 'Cc-ed' your political contenders, your loudest supporters jeer...?

Well, it's because YOU are MY president.
It's because YOU are the master goldsmith of this era.
It's because, YOU are the Captain of MY ship.
And I'd hate to believe that:
MY President cannot lead me,

That MY Master Goldsmith has lost his midas touch, nimble fingers and eye for delicate beauty,

That MY Captain is oblivious to the coordinates that will lead to our promised land of destination...

And above all, it's because Ghana, this HUSTLER'S PARADISE, is by no means any kind of a paradise for an ambitious GHANAIAN woman of creative dissidence, like me.

Yours sincerely,
Apiorkor Seyiram Ashong
(An Ambitious Ghanaian Woman of Creative Dissidence)
2016

HUSTLER'S PARADISE – WE STILL LIVE HERE

Dear Your Excellency Nana Addo Dankwa Akufo-Addo,

Allow me to begin by saying that I do respect and admire you, immensely.

Unlike many Ghanaians, I believe that our president; regardless of our individual political affiliations and sentiments; deserves our respect. After all, being the Head of State of a nation could not possibly be a walk in the park.

Having said this, though, you must not take it to necessarily mean that I identify with and glorify the political ideologies and practices that characterise and depict the political colours of your divide.

Additionally, quite frankly, none of your known political contenders has proven to me that his or her camp would make a SIGNIFICANTLY better alternative for the Ghana that I love so deeply.

However, lately, Ghana has become a HUSTLER'S PARADISE. The trouble with this is that, albeit I am an ambitious Ghanaian woman of creative dissidence, the fact remains that I was not born to HUSTLE.

Therefore, I am an unhappy Ghanaian, at the moment. My ambition is bathed in filthy, gooey, smelly, revolting, mucous-y spittle.

My creativity is stunted, because I am forced to give so much of the maximum, just so that I can attain the bare minimum. The foundation of my dissidence is shaken. I have lost my way. I am losing myself. My days are full of a blazing sun that feeds off of the migraine that has become the plague of my brain. My spirit is broken and I kneel, I pray, I hope, I speak prosperity into my life, and into the seemingly infertile womb of Ghana.

I have tried to channel my ambition, creativity and dissidence into a single, massive ball of an adrenaline-charged HUSTLE!

But, Your Excellency, I was not born to HUSTLE.

Seeing as I believe in giving people the chance to prove themselves to be different from what public and mass perceptions and conceptions might convey,

I would be most grateful, Your Excellency, if you would let me know how you can help to (in the least) mitigate the effects of this predicament, within which I find myself.

And why do I ask you, you say?

Why have I not 'Cc-ed' your political contenders, your loudest supporters jeer...?

Well, it's because YOU are MY president.
It's because YOU are the master goldsmith of this era.
It's because, YOU are the Captain of MY ship.
And I'd hate to believe that:
MY President cannot lead me,

That MY Master Goldsmith has lost his midas touch, nimble fingers and eye for delicate beauty,

That MY Captain is oblivious to the coordinates that will lead to our promised land of destination...

And above all, it's because Ghana, this HUSTLER'S PARADISE, is by no means any kind of a paradise for an ambitious GHANAIAN woman of creative dissidence, like me.

Yours sincerely,
Apiorkor Seyiram Ashong
(An Ambitious Ghanaian Woman of Creative Dissidence)
2019

A TALE OF SURVIVAL

She knew where she had come from; her family had made many sacrifices for her to get an education.
Her siblings stayed at home, because her parents could pay school fees, for only one child at a time.
Then Free SHS came; they all went to school, but they still had to buy school uniforms, provisions, sanitary pads – things which were still difficult for their parents to afford.

Yet, they were able to survive.
She worked hard, when she was in high school…
She earned seven A's and one B and she was certain that she would be able to become the first person in her family, to obtain a University degree. But there is no money.

And what would it take to be able to survive?
- Hawking on the streets of Accra?
- Working as a kayayo, with the possibility of being cheated by selfish customers during the day or raped by ruthless predators at night?
- Spending a steamy night with an older woman, even though she doesn't really swing that way?
- Stealing from that majestic house, with the gigantic gate?
- Or having to depend on the benevolence of a rich boyfriend, in return for favours which we cannot speak of?

Please help her to find some solace of honey in life's beehive…
Please help her to survive.

2019

CHOICES III

Every woman should have a choice, even if it means that choice is an abortion.
I always say that I do not know what I would do, if I were to find myself in certain situations;
I do not know if my choice would be to have an abortion, or not.
I know so many women, who are unhappy with their lives and they take their frustration out on their children.
Many of those women say that societal pressure guilted them into choosing to keep their pregnancies, as opposed to having an abortion.
As for rape victims and abortions; again it's a woman's choice.
And again I have seen rape victims, rape survivors who abuse their innocent kids,
be it by beating them mercilessly and at the least provocation,
by burning them with hot, smouldering charcoal,
by leaving them to sleep on the sandy, ant-infested ground, while mosquitoes feast on their young and tender flesh,
by selling them to the highest bidder, in Accra, or Kumasi – the money is later used to pay for the latest hairdo, or the flashiest cell phone,
And even
by sexually traumatising and mutilating them…
Why do the mothers in question do these horrendous things?
Well, it's because they never had the chance to project all of their pent-up anger, shame, hatred and frustration onto the people who abused, or raped them.
And guess what – you and I most likely don't even know that such a woman was abused, or raped.

Contrastingly, other women love their kids to bits and have risen above all of their fear, trauma and rage:
They bathe their children three times a day,
Babies suckle from their breasts, while they look down at them, their eyes heavy with a blazing love.
They starve, that those whom their wombs birthed shall eat and be filled.
And they love their little ones, until it hurts, because they love them so hard that it bruises their insides…!
Bottom line: The world is just too judgmental.
By all means, laws and structures are necessary, in order to protect humanity from itself;
But some of us are squares and others are circles, apples and oranges –
And we cannot always live by a one-size-fits-all philosophy and especially not when it comes to something as sensitive and as weighty as the issue of abortion.

2019

The Experience Of The Ghanaian Woman

ENTRAPMENT OF AGONY

Agony...
I tried to deal with it, but I couldn't.
I tried. I tried. I said I tried!

So, before you look me in the eye and ask me to calm down.
Before you project your myopic preconceptions onto my actions and inactions.

Before you ask me not to give up, because you've crowned yourself chief motivator of the century.
Before you call me a quitter, you judgmental hypocrite of a human being...

Know that I was trapped. The wheel kept moving, but I couldn't move, because I was trapped.

The wheel kept turning and turning, tugging at those spiritual strings that kept digging the grave of my life.

And I struggled. I fought. I punched. I kicked, I bit, I spat.
I TRIED, can't you hear me?!

But he shot bullets of excruciating agony, into me...
I was entrapped and I tried to get out and I failed...

But I will fail at this, only but once.

2016

THAT NIGHT I LOST MY WALLET

Stunning lady; fixated eyes, lost wallet.

The thick, silky, shiny, coily, curly hair.

That black dress that clung to her outlines, as though she had immersed and drenched her hills and valleys in therapeutic sea waters, on a breezy harmattan night.

Forget the dress; it was the nooks, crannies, hills, valleys and ridges of her caramel frame that drove me crazy.

She flounced past me; no, her perfect breasts flounced past me.

And those pelvic regions swayed in a fiery frenzy.

Then I caught a glimpse of the two perfect oval loaves of fresh bread that hid beneath the clingy black dress. A living, breathing, perfect mannequin, complete with all of the best of feminine humanity!

Then it was time to pay for my meal and my drinks…

Stunning lady; fixated eyes, lost wallet.

2015

LASTFRIDAY

Friday: ampesi, bolognese, kelewele, candles, fudge.
Kisses... Darkness.
But it wasn't a hollow, stale, heavy kind of darkness.
It was that kind of darkness that envelopes you, the kind that is atmosphered by the lingering tastes of good food.
It was the kind of darkness that is injected with the desirable smokey-vanilla-strawberry aroma of candles, whose flames died long ago, because two sets of devouring lips, together, have cut off the air supply.
It was a kind of darkness that was stained with shiny moon powder, just enough of it to accentuate the thick, full lips,
the banana-cherry-peachy beams of skin,
the mass of silky coils,
the breasts that stand-fall kissable...

And I made sure that I bent this way and that, so that my curves could bounce off the moon powder, at the right angles;
at the softest angles;
at the most alluring angles...

Then he became almost innocent in his vulnerability and that's when I knew that I loved this new kind of darkness; this sensual, sweaty, moony, touchy, candle-laced, weird-but-sexily-delicious-smelling kind of darkness.
It was only the beginning...
Fridays: ampesi, bolognese, kelewele, candles, fudge.
Kisses... Darkness.

2015

THE MONGREL

Undress Me!

My lips are thick and full, although smaller than the alluring marshmallows that sit on Asabea's and Ama's faces.

My eyes are dough-y saucers and my skin emits banana-cherry-peachy beams that do something of what a hologram does in the sun's eyes.
My hair is a mass of silky coils; not cake-ily kinky like afro hair is supposed to be.
My breasts stand-fall kissable and the skin of my butt, my hips and my thighs ripples when my foot meets the ground.

So they call me an obroni, a white woman: I am not African enough. I could not possibly be Ghanaian.

Undress me, I say!

I am not a big fan of fufu and light soup and goat meat and snails.
My colleagues, at work, say that I'm showy and elitist, because I make meals of chicken noodles and cinnamon rolls.
They mock my accent, calling it foreign and bourgeois.

I am an educated, career woman. I work long hours and I embrace my sexuality. I flaunt my dewy cleavage and I join men in conversations about wild, casual sex and sensual foreplay, erotic role-play.

I voice my candid opinions on politics and the sweet and sour socioeconomic buffet that we find ourselves eating from: I argue. I scream.

But they say women must talk less and listen more. We are meant to be admired (and by this they mean we are meant to be looked at with bulging eyes that cut us up to our privates and eat us, before we can be cooked). They say women mustn't talk about sex and should cover their assets – better to imagine them, than to see them. They say that I am Westernised and must learn to be more of an Ama or an Asabea, because I am an Apiorkor…

And if they undressed me, beyond the heavy, supple breasts, after kissing the fiery lips, when the hips, thighs and butt have ravished and have been ravished; they'd find that the flesh and blood are laden with various genotypes of various records, eras, spaces and love children…

2014

NO ROOM HERE

I. Feel. Bad.

Last night, Kofi Asamoah asked me to marry him, and I said no.

Last week, Kofi Asamoah took me shopping and now my wardrobe is a dam, bursting with colourful waterfalls.

Last month, Kofi Asamoah drew a kiss on my lips, while he entrenched a key into my sweaty palm.

And now my arms jiggle and my stomach bulges with milky flesh, after all, I hardly walk anymore.

Last year, Kofi Asamoah carried me in his arms, as his molten fingers brushed at the skin beneath my rear cheeks. I clung to his shiny, melting neck and tossed my head backwards, in typical girlish delight.

Then he kissed my forehead and my eyes and my nose and my hair, as we entered the foyer of the duplex. Then we explored each other on a blanket on the cold kitchen floor.

Last year, Last month, Last week;

Kofi Asamoah was here.

With me. Loving me. Spoiling me...

I. Feel. Bad.

Last night Kofi Asamoah asked me to marry him; and I said no.

Because there is no room here,

Not in my head

Not in my heart

Not in my soul

Not in my life...

2014

TO FORSAKEN LOVE

I once walked upon a red carpet.
I was surrounded by pink, yellow, blue, red... A garden of flowers.
My neck was adorned with a necklace of gold.
My hair was coloured with delicate water lilies, white to signify purity and happiness.

My fingers dazzled in the sun- kissed breeze.
And my feet were oiled with a sweetly- scented parfum.
A dress of silk and honey- yellow clasped my frame;
I felt beautiful and I believed I looked beautiful.
The crown of it all was not my glistening tiara, but the Halo that encased my heart.
The one that HE placed there.
He LOVED me... or at least I thought he did.
My heart was ripe for him and he plucked it. He embalmed it with his healing salve.
And my wounds were soothed,
And they got better, gradually, until no scars remained...
And then, I was happy again.
At that point I should have been snapped back into reality.
I should have lost all vulnerabilities to you,
I should have lost all dependency upon you.
But I was a fool!
I let my guard down and I became a simpleton.
For it was at that very point that you began to imprint a deeper, redder, more painful wound upon my heart.
And now, a gaping hole is what I have to show for a fairytale romance.

Now, all I have is memories.

No more necklaces.

No more flowers.

No more sun.

No more tiaras.

No more lilies.

No more dresses or delicate parfums and oils.

No more love.

No more passion...

I do not regret, ever welcoming you into my life, into my world, into my very being!

But, Oh!

How I wish our fairytale could have remained as such!

For my heart, it once beat for you.

And it now bleeds for the lack of you.

I pray you remain Happy and Blessed,

For I love you and wouldn't pray for anything less.

Yet, you must know that for every drop of blood that escapes my battered heart;

You will receive a grave punishment, from Aphrodite, the good goddess of love...

2008

DRIZZLE

Touch me. The dew of your caressing-finger-tips glazes the small of my back. You lay it on, thick as cold honey and smooth as warm liquid-milk-choco-late. Then the inner me journeys to realms of fire and ice, stone and lava...

Hold me. The hair on your massive arms tickles me silly, with a feather-light stroke, here and there and I giggle; and giggle; breathe. Giggle and giggle-giggle-giggle; breathe-breathe-breathe. Giggle and giggle, until I can breathe no more...

Love me. The kisses that you steal throw me into a whirlwind of ecstatic, electrically charged and explosive atoms; they throw me this way and that way, upwards, they push me downwards, so that I remain in my own little, yet expansive capsule, forever a slave to your raw energy.

Then you smother me with so much tenderness, so much un-hinged emotion that my heart and soul yearn… for you...
And at the instance that I declare my unflinching allegiance to you;
At the very stroke of the hour, when I throw my hands up in utter relinquishment;
At the very moment that your ocean seems to have engulfed me... I will not falter. I will not drown. But I will drink in all the beautiful elements of your powerful ocean of love; the cold honey & the warm liquid-milk-chocolate; the fire, the ice; the stone & the lava...
I will gulp your salt waters down and loose myself in my incessant fits of hairy, feathery-induced giggles.

And when I have ingested every drop of your ocean-potion, we will become one...

Then I no longer feel restricted by your ocean, for it is now a part of me and the droplets of that ocean of yours will be but a drizzle as we walk hand-in-hand, side-by-side, for all of eternity.

2014

TO LOVE

I had oft than not spent my time with myself.
I was self-absorbed and self-indulgent.
I had not the time for anything or anyone-

And my heart was encased in glass and crystal.
No one could touch it, or to do so much as whisper to it.
It was safe, inaccessible.
And my case of glass and crystal was unbreakable.
And the seconds, minutes, hours, days, months and years would pass me by, and my little, beating heart would remain safe and healthy.

No...no one could touch it.
No...no man could come along and break it.
He could only gaze at it through the transparent walls of its sturdy case of crystal and glass...
Little did I know that, as all those seconds, minutes, hours, days, months and years passed me by, passed my heart by; passed us by; this heart of mine grew colder and sadder, and turned bluer by the hour.
For, you see,
I did not realise that:
That my heart dwells within my bosom, but SHE has a mind and a heart of her own.
And I really had no control...
And HE came along, on tip-toe,
with controlled and silenced breathing...

Then suddenly, and without so much as a red flag, my beautiful
encasement of crystal and fine
glass had been shattered,
and he was breathing a new life into my dear heart...
You see
you can protect the heart from pain, but you cannot hide the heart
from the power and determination of the thing called LOVE!

2009

FATE & REALITY

I used to catch my mommy crying over the family's pot of Sunday, buttered-lamb stew.

Her eyes kept inflating, until they looked like bofroat

Then her eyesight got bad and it was all the crying that was the problem.

I recall how my puerile brain absorbed the stories about my grandma's illness, after she had finally discovered that grandpa had two children; they didn't come from her womb. "She almost went mad," the stories would end, inadvertently.

I was moulded with the notions that "women are forever loyal" and that "young ladies should search for men who are loyal to their mothers and sisters, because they'd be less likely to cheat".

But in my early 20's, the young men would kiss my lips with their lying lips, suck my nipples with their lying tongues, then steal away into the cover of darkness.

Then at daybreak, the village gong-gong beater would announce that some other women had been licking the young men's love-parts in the night. Then I cried, until my eyes looked like bofroat.

And now, every woman knows that she must accept a hard fate; all men will kiss her lips with their lying lips, suck her nipples with their lying tongues, then steal away into another woman's cloth, under the cover of darkness.

And now, every man knows that no woman will cry; no woman will get sick and have a close encounter with madness. She will just go and lick another man's love-parts at night. And he will suck her nipples with his lying tongue and lick her love-parts.

So, I ask myself, were my mommy's tears indicative of her failure to accept her fate? Did my grandma's illness creep upon her, while she was hiding from a reality?

Or maybe they had accepted their fate, all along, and their human nature could not contain the reality.

Perhaps women of today saw their mommies' tears and heard their grandmas' stories; and now we've become vengeful and careless with love-parts.

2015

TO SUMMER... A BEAUTIFUL AFFAIR

 I can see a white beach,
The sands as pure, as breath taking as a newborn's smile and cry...

I flirt with the idea of holding your hand,
Being lifted up off the ground, so that my longing lips meet yours
in a mind-wrecking explosion...

I laugh.
I laugh my heart out till I cry.
Because in you 'Summer', I've found a peculiar joy.
Even as I whispered harmless rhymes to you at night
Over the phone,
Beneath the lamp-post's seductive aura of soft light...
My girlish imagination toyed with the idea of being in your arms;
You caressed my cheeks,
You stroked my hair,
You smoothed those masculine fingers down my hips...
Oh! Summer!
I blush, even at the thought of it all,
So that my cheeks burn as hot and as bright as your companion;
the sun.
Then I go to bed each hot Summer's night;
My body burning from your heat,
Yet I wish that the heat was initiated by your warm kisses on my
neck and bosom...
A heat, escalated by your own dear presence beside me;
As we turn over the questions in our heads:
"Should I ask Summer to stay?"

OR
"Should I give way to 'Cold Autumn'?"
"Should I ask her to pick berries from my stock?"
OR
"Should I let her go?"
Truth is,
I love Summer.
I'd like to experience the fusion of us two,
For my star is Aries as fiery as your sun.
Then I'd love to play with your leaves,
Imagine them to be your gorgeous hair.
Then I'd love for you, Summer, to devour me, as though
You were a wicked forest fire, ravishing any beautiful maple or
weeping willow in its path.
Then, finally, we'd resurface and lay – body to heart and heart to
soul –
And I'd awake upon the beach,
wishing that you'd look at me, the way you look at the picturesque
picnic lay-out that you've set for us two,
Kindred spirits, near the
rolling waters that wash away my fantasy...
On a hot Summer's evening.
"It was definitely a beautiful affair, while it lasted…"

2008

LIP PRAYER

Your lips are mine and mine are yours.

May my lips forever glorify and honour you.
May my lips be truthful to you.
May my lips calm your blazing brow and bring healing to your aching muscles.
May my lips mop up your tears.
May my lips dry the sweat of your toil, from your chest.
May my lips defend you, when the law fails and when friends and family forsake you.
May my lips raise you from the ground, when you cannot walk.
May you find nourishment in my lips, when you cannot afford to buy food.
May my lips be your most expensive and most preferred dessert.
May my lips quench your thirst.
May my lips be the light unto your darkest path.
May you find solace in my lips.
May you yearn for my lips.
May my lips always profess my love for you...

Your lips were made for me and mine for you.

And may my lips forever bear testimony of the bitter-sweet beauty that is our union, our love.

2017

SISTER BLEEDS

You sit there and you waste away in pain.

You lie in bed and your spirit aches.

You show your teeth, yet they paint but a ghost-smile.

You take beautiful pictures that are thick with ugly secrets.

You walk through your office corridors with two masks on your face; the well-done, expensive makeup and your poker face.

Your hair is freshly pressed, intricately curled, it's a mass of long, luscious locks and it's yours, because you bought it. But the real catch is the HD video that plays in your hair's glossy finish, an endless motion picture of you moaning and groaning and tossing your legs over your head, while he sprays wads of legal tender into you, the ones that you push out to get your hair done.

You show up at every party, every fundraiser, every wedding, every social gathering that's worth talking about and you seem to solve everyone's needs; to the world you're the quintessential social butterfly, but all you really are is an attention seeker, because attention isn't what you crave, it's what you need.

You dance in Church, because the Faith tells you that you are supposed to be grateful for God's faithfulness, but tell me, what faith do you truly have in your heart?

You take Uber and Taxi rides through the city: Circle, Airport, Spintex, East Legon, Dansoman, Lapaz, Ridge, Adabraka, Osu, La, Nungua, Teshie. Forget the trotro! – but your salary is barely enough and you live for your boyfriend's cedis and that rich man's dollars.

You kiss his lips and stroke his hair and massage his temples and plan a dream wedding and take him into you and moan for him; but he'll never be man enough for you. Your love for him can never be unconditional and pure, because it fluctuates with each bank account deposit that he makes and every word of adoration that comes out of a better man's mouth.

You lie by his side and wish:

that the rich man were yours,

that the handsome man would make a sweet mistake and caress you just once,

that the caring man would make you breakfast after you'd have lured him to a long night of passion,

that the married man would have married you,

that the Whatsapp man would give you physical quivers, instead of virtual kisses and that   he might actually mean it, when he types 'I love you.'

Your friends envy you: How did you do it, how do you do it? You are so blessed. You are so pretty. You slay every day. You have such a supportive family. You have such a good man. You are living the good life.

But your very lonely existence feels cursed with the façade that has become your reality.

So…

To You, I say it's okay to hurt.

To You, I say your spirit can be mended.

To You, I say that it's only a strong woman who smiles, as her heart hemorrhages.

To You, I say that taking beautiful pictures can help to heal a broken soul.

To You, I say that masks of makeup and poker faces are fine; what goes on in your life is none of the world's business.

To You, I say that your existence need not depend on a fleet of men sailing in and out of your delicate waters, but never docking at your harbour.

To You, I say that love can exist, as you imagine it and as your soul needs it to be.

To You, I say that there are people who can see through your façade and read you like they would a good book; they watch your movie silently and without judgment, while they keep you in their prayers.

To You, I say that sometimes it's good to talk to such people and to learn from them, because it's okay to hurt, but pain masked for too long eats you up and kills you slowly…

And to all the women, who have lost hope and have begun to feel that they tread the path of this treacherous world alone,

To You, I say that you have a bleeding sister in me.

2017

DAWN

Wake up!
Heart beats.
Sweat engulfs me.
My mind is in overdrive... I look up.
I look to the left.
I look to the right.
One glance backwards.
I look straight ahead... I can recall how I used to sit in a quiet corner of our picturesque home in Easton, Pennsylvania.
I would suck my thumb and grasp a book with the other hand.
Then every now and then, I would give my thumb a break and sip hot chocolate from my little yellow "cocoa cup". I can see myself in the 2nd grade play, singing my 8-year-old heart out.

I can feel myself gliding up and down our driveway, in a fierce rollerblading battle.
I can see years of joy and hurt...
The pillar of life that is my mother.
The heartbeat that is my father.
The sisters who define SISTERHOOD.
The family that paints my blood.
The friends who are really just family in disguise.
The mongrel that I am- American, Ghanaian, Ga, Ewe, Akuapem.
The falls and scrapes that came with being a tomboy.
The academic milestones.
The world trips.
The Accra club parties at Boomerang, Pier One and The Warehouse.

The loves that I loved deeply.
The loves whose love I wasn't worthy of.
The passion of doing a job that I love.
The crack-high that Poetry injects me with.
The soul mate who intoxicates me with endless doses of love, life and lovemaking and who gives another dimension of meaning to the concept of LOVE, in the first place.

Wake up!
Heart beats.
Sweat engulfs me.
My mind is in overdrive... I look up.
I look to the left.
I look to the right.
One glance backwards.
I look straight ahead... What I see all around is beautiful.
What I see is a rich blueprint of my life, complete with the flaws and renovations.

But what I see when I look straight ahead is another life with you.
And now that you're here in the flesh,
Now that we've begun the next phase of this journey that God never promised would be easy,
Now that you're helpless in grasp and seek my reassurance with every one of your intense gazes:

We will travel these winding paths,
Looking straight ahead
And leaving a deep, heavy footprint with each confident step... For wherever I look,

Be it up, left, right or backwards;
All I see is what's ahead with you.

2017

GIRLS, WOMEN, FRIENDS

Irreplaceable friends...
Women of wisdom.
Women of God.
Women of influence.
Women of diligence.
Women of class.
Women of exposure.
Women of experience.
Women of perseverance.
Women of admirable humility.
Women of outstanding intellect.
Women of Love.
Women of grace.
Women of intense industry.
Women of maturity.
Women who are agents of positive societal change.
Women who have grown to become my sisters.
Women who have been there for over a decade.
Women who were once girls, but have traversed life's thick forests into womanhood, all the while making my own journey much more bearable.
And they remain in the vessel, as I sail through the first waves of the waters of motherhood.

2017

THANKFULTONGUE

When the Lord blesses you with the strength to keep on pushing
And to work harder than ever,
When another human being is growing inside of you, you can't be
ungrateful about it and complain all the time.
So cheers to the swollen feet,
the aching joints,
the insomnia
and the incessant fatigue!
I'm going to keep on conquering you all, God be my helper!

And Piggy, I could never have had a better partner through it all.
You, Sir, are a rare and phenomenal gem.

2017

DANCING LEGEND

You were born to dance, my love, yes, you were born to dance.

The legend of your life has it that,
At one point when your mother was seven months pregnant with
you - you were still.
The legend says that you were so still that your mother got
alarmed.
She thought you were dead!

That night, your mother wept.
The legend told that she cried so hard, with deep, raspy coughs
coming from her throat, through her mouth and thick, yellow
mucous came out too.

That night, your father was a ghost
The legend told that he couldn't breathe properly and that Dede
ran in and out of the bedroom
Several times
With several glasses of water.
Your father almost fainted that night, watching as your mother's
condition deteriorated and as all of the drama and endless crying
began to make her bleed from between her legs and her eyes got
pale and she could no longer scream, no longer mourn her unborn
child.

That night both your mother and father were rushed to the
hospital by a neighbour.
That night the doctor put your father on a drip.

That night the doctor induced your mother's labour, while a small radio near what had become her bed of suffering and sorrow, played a classic, upbeat highlife tune...
And that night, as your father groaned in pain, as your mother howled in agony, as the doctors were like flies on rotting mangoes

You danced.
You danced in your mother's womb.
You danced to that classic, upbeat highlife tune that came from the radio.
The Legend told that your mother's excruciating pain turned to unquenchable joy and that your father was proud and that the doctors rejoiced.
Then you were born and you moved to the reggae beats that were playing now.

You were conceived to dance, the Legend said;
You were born to dance...

And over the years, you have danced with me;
Rubbing me with your sweaty chest,
Loving me with your gyrating hips,
Caressing me with your roaming hands,
Embracing me in your loving and caring arms...

And I have danced with you;
Willingly swaying my hips to the melody in your head,
Bumping my bum against you behind me,
Grabbing your hands and arms and holding them tightly, while they explore my curves.

You were born to dance with me, the legend says:
And dancing with you has never felt as wonderful as it does now;
I'll dance with you now and always.

2017

LOVE SAVED ME

There was a time when I couldn't look you in the eye.

There was a time when I feared to sit in your presence;

Heck, there was a time when I trembled at the thought of placing my foot in your footprint!

But time doesn't stand still.

So, today I stomp on your deepest footprint.

Today, a table is set before me, in your very presence; and I drink from a goblet of gold and diamonds, while you sip from a wooden tumbler.

Today, I stand before you and I look, squarely, into both of your eyes, then I look away, then I look at you again; into your deep, dark, daggered eyes... You may have beaten me on all of those rainy nights.

You may have torn my red panties, yes, the ones that you asked me to wear, just so that you could tear them to shreds, to prove to me that you could buy red lingerie over and over again.

And you may have bruised my soul, stabbed my spirit, broken my nose, teeth-marked my breasts and swollen my lips... But I have found the one, whom my soul loves:

And love has saved me, love has healed me, love has elevated my status!

And because of love,

you will be blinded by the gleam in my eyes,

you will eat the crumbs from my table,

you will trip over my hefty footprints... And I will always over-power you with powerful love.

2016

PENSIVE WOMAN

In my world there's me...

But then there's you and when I bask in the moon light of my globe, I find myself yearning for a little more of you... Just a little more;

Because I need you tonight, and maybe for always.

2016

THE HONEY POT

Amina soaps up her breasts, her thighs and her derriere.

Amina squats and washes her honey pot; it doesn't produce much honey these days.

Amina washes the suds from her hair and skin. She has used the expensive rose-scented bath oil that Fiifi gave to her on her birthday. He likes it.

Amina dries herself off. Amina moves sluggishly, trudges on to THE room. Amina slathers something coconutty onto her breasts, her stomach, her thighs, her feet...

Now; Amina must wait...

Fiifi loves his wife, but she will not conceive. He needs his male child; little Bella is not enough; a man-child will marry her and his name will be lost.

But Amina will not get pregnant.

Fiifi shoves his man-stick into her honey pot and thrusts and wiggles and thrusts. Amina cannot feel the movement. She cannot feel the blood slithering down her chunky thighs. Now, she's dead down there.

Amina used to scream, but no one came. Amina used to fight, but Fiifi would only shove and thrust; shove and thrust harder. He didn't care that her honey pot no longer secreted honey. He was oblivious to the thick, red blotches of viscous blood-honey that replaced the honey.

Amina soaps up her breasts, her thighs and her derriere; Amina squats and washes her honey pot, which only produces blood-honey these days.

Amina washes the shame and pain from her skin and Fiifi's sticky spittle from her mane.

Then she trudges on to THE room to lay by his side, praying that tonight, at 2.00 am, she is already with male child; or at least some baby, who will be the Saviour to end a Madonna's mortal misery.

2015

BORN OF A WAVE OF EMOTION

Light that candle, my love… For it is only when you do, that you
will see, ever so clearly, just how luminous our love becomes when
ignited:
'Tis rather strange.

I awoke this morning with a distinct yearning for you;
With an inexplicable intoxication of my senses – you were there.
Yet, you were not there.
I was confused.
'Twas rather strange.

So, born of a wave of intense emotion, here is a song for you;
A song I have sung to you over the years.
A song that has tickled your ears in a different language each time,
And yet the lyrics remain as the fruits of Eden,
As poisonous and murderous as a woman's love for her man could
be…

This song has told you many things.

Never forget, my love, the overwhelming sensation that has often
encased you through my song;
Cast your mind back to the voluminous scars the sensation left
after it
scalded your forehead,
scalded the soles of your feet,
scalded your smooth, dark, beautiful skin,
scalded your groin… yes

Cast your mind back to the scars that this sensation created, with every vow of the genuine love of the one that you claim to love; and pay particular attention to the one lonesome bruise that lies deep within your bosom, the centre of your love for her.

Yes, this song has told you many things.

Recall, my dear, each vivid mental image that my tune has ever engraved upon your mind.
Ruminate upon the sweet pain that those images of
luscious breasts,
ample hips and thighs,
lips ablaze from your fiery kisses,
warm nakedness of the one whom you claim to love… yes
Ruminate on the sweet pain that those images have put you through.
For you loved to feast your eyes upon those images, even as they initiated a sudden, painful rushing of blood within you.

Yes, this song has told you many things:

Reminisce for dear life and love, on each moment of arousal and passion that you so willingly shared with the one you love, as she laid her melody, thick as honey, deep within your left and right ear canals.
Get re- acquainted with those moments, during which
You never took your eyes off of her, as she entered the room,
You undressed her with your eyes, You moaned and groaned at the very caress of her fingertips,
You clasped her hips firmly, adjoining it to your groin,
You felt her breath in your ear, along with the melody,

You rid her of every article of clothing,
You kissed every nook and cranny of her aroused body,
You picked her up, and placed her on a bed of red and black silk,
colours as POISONOUS as she
You milked her,
You explored her body with your hands, and tongue...YES
Get re-acquainted with those moments, during which, like a predator does to its prey, you nudged her bosom, you tickled her nipples with your tongue, you savoured the feel of her burning flesh against yours, so that you both melted to become one...

But pay particular attention to the powerful image of the smell of her shampoo as you held her earlobe between your teeth; the scent of her dew-garden that pricked at your nose, as you entered her, the fragrance of the liquid that poured from her pores, as you drove her to a mind-wrecking climax:

Each instance shall remain with her for all time...

'Tis rather strange.

I awoke this morning with a song for you,
The words creating a quiver on my lips...

My love, as you make an effort to cast your mind back, as you ruminate on the sweet pain,
As you get re-acquainted with those erotic, erupting, volcanic moments...

Keep that candle a-kindle, my love...
For I handed it to you as I lavished you with the first notes of my
dynamic song,
And when I did, I knew it was only when you lighted it, that you
would see just how luminous our love becomes when ignited:
Because, that candle burned unceasingly in our first spasms of
erotic passion.

2008

BEAUTY KNOWS NO SHAME

A new kind of beauty to embrace and celebrate.
There's no room for shame here.

There's a power that pushes through from within,
There's a power that will push out and bring my bloody insides
with it...
But that's something of a pain that I'd love to succumb to, in a
natural, agony-sedating, physical rage.

I'm learning that weakness isn't always weakness, that weakness
can eat you up in a beautiful and majestic way.

And that weakness can make you fall in love
with pain,
with drunken fatigue,
with needles that spit things into you and
with pins that suck and draw reddish-purplish blood from you,
with bleeding gums,
with aching joints,
with vomit and
with a buffet of other revolting things.

And the seemingly-breathless lungs keep you in a perpetual gasp,
as though you yourself were swimming through a watery fluid
made of electrolytes, proteins, carbohydrates, lipids, urea and
other things that take me back to my high school Biology lab.

It's apparently ugly, but miraculously gorgeous:

It's a new kind of beauty to embrace and to celebrate.
And there is no room for shame here.

Just pride and strange things and a new me.

2017

THOUGHTS OF A SLAVE

I'm sitting here, drinking in the colours of our son's
face, while he eats his fill from my left breast...

I'm pretty much naked, in my black panties of French
lace and my nude-coloured maternity bra.
My back is propped up by pillows, against the head
of my parents' antique bed frame.
I notice that the mask of pregnancy is gradually dissolving,
my stomach isn't charcoal-black and
chalky-feeling anymore – it's beginning to match the
rest of my body.
I see that the stretch marks on my heavy, supple
breasts are fading and they shine when the sunlight
in the window tries to kiss my milky nipples.
I find that my body is fuller, softer, more motherly.
And I can't help but wonder if you find me as attractive
as you used to...

Then my mind wanders to a place, which seems to be
light years away.
I remember that first phone call. I heard your voice and
it warmed my heart, even though it was the voice of a
stranger. And somehow, I felt as though I knew that
voice.

You were enslaving me and I was oblivious to it...

I recall the countless text messages and phone calls

that this faceless Man rained on me. I began to
look forward to them.

You were enslaving me and I was oblivious to it...
And I cannot forget the first day that I set my eyes
on your beautiful face. It was such a refreshing
experience.

You were enslaving me and I was oblivious to it...
My mind shows me images of the first night that we
spent together, you held me tightly while my forehead
was saturated with pain, agony.
You attempted to kiss the pain away and rocked me to
sleep, as though I were your baby girl.

You were enslaving me and I was oblivious to it...
I'm slapped with warmth, as I relive the heat of the
moment when we first made love.
You touched me with passion, yet with so much
meaning. I felt the love seep through your fingertips,
as you caressed my back, my thighs, my stomach, as
you rubbed and stroked me down there...
you rubbed and stroked me down there...
I can feel your tongue on the tips of my nipples, as I
remember how you suckled them, as though your life
depended on it.
And I recall thinking that I never wanted your manhood
to let go of my lady parts, because it felt so real, so
hot, so true, so good; I wished that we could make love
24/7; you were the best that I'd ever had, the first man
to take me into an orgasmic realm...

You were enslaving me and I was oblivious to it…
My eyes tear up, as I picture all of the times that
you've stared at me with intensity, so much so that I
could feel your love encasing me, almost choking me,
intoxicating me.

You were enslaving me and I was oblivious to it…
I look back at all of the times that you've held me,
made me cry, wiped my tears, sexed me silly and I
know that you were made for me!

I'm sitting here, drinking in the colours of our son's
face, while he eats his fill from my left breast…

I'm pretty much naked, in my black panties of French
lace and my nude-coloured maternity bra.
My back is propped up by pillows, against the head
of my parents' antique bed frame.
And I recall a time when we couldn't afford to have a
child; painful and emotionally draining abortions were
the answer.
A time when I miscarried and began to question
whether I'd ever be able to bear your child.
A time when our present, as husband and wife, was
but a dream, a wish, something that we worked
towards every single day…
You enslaved me and I was oblivious to it…

I notice that the mask of pregnancy is gradually dissolving,
my stomach isn't charcoal-black and
feeling chalky anymore – it's beginning to match the
rest of my body.

I see that the stretch marks on my heavy, supple
breasts are fading and they shine when the sunlight
in the window tries to kiss my milky nipples.
I find that my body is fuller, softer, more motherly.
And I can't help but wonder if you find me as attractive
as you used to...

Because today,
I see your face in our love child, the fruit of my womb.
I see my beauty in his countenance.
I see your love for me, in his love for me.
And I'm reminded that
So much time has passed,
So much has changed,
We've grown in so many ways;
You've enslaved me in countless ways;
But my love for you is unshaken, unchanged, unadulterated...
And I still want to pounce on you and ride your groin
with fiery passion, anytime that I set my eyes upon you...

And I still believe that no other man can hold a torch to
your perfection, as
A lover,
A friend,
A husband,
Even as a man...

And I ask that you forgive the incoherence of my
thoughts and words, because
I'm sitting here, drinking in the colours of our son's
face, while he eats his fill from my left breast...

And I'm confused and overwhelmed and excited by the emotional heritage with which his father has enslaved me – The Emotional Heritage of love.

2018

A BOW FOR THE WOMAN

Tonight, I sit in my hotel room in Takoradi and watch
the waves of the Atlantic Ocean that kiss Ghana's feet.
Fragments of my life before the cameras, float to me
and then away from me, with the ebb and flow of the
monstrous water currents...
Tonight, is the night that I'll be celebrated as a queen of
the screen, for the last time.
Tonight, I'll wiggle into a body-hugging bespoke gown,
just once more.
Tonight, I'll strut down the red carpet of Ghanaian
film, in six-inch heels, and then I won't look back at my
footprints, because that door would be closed, my trail
hidden.
Tonight, I'll smile for the cameras just one last time...
No more movies,
No more 18-hour road trips, from Accra to Kumasi,
through Sunyani to Tamale, to Navrongo, back to Peki,
over to Elmina, back to Accra,
No more late moonlit nights and early sunlit mornings
spent
Striving to get into character,
Striving to escape,
Striving to rid myself of personal values, beliefs and
preconceptions,
Striving so hard;
To become some other woman,
To become someone else...
To become someone else...

July, 1970...

"Take it off!" the director yelled at me.

With tears in my eyes, I took my blouse off.

This wasn't the plan, but he said that I had to experience sexual harassment, in order to be able to act as though I'd been sexually harassed.

But I endured the humiliation, because I knew that I had to send a message to the world about my suffering; about the suffering of many Ghanaian women.

And I was elated when by the end of 1970, that movie had encouraged 37 women to speak up about their encounters with rape, about their sleazy bosses, about their rape-children!

37 women had been inspired by me, a nobody who got lucky, because I was "sexy" and "pretty" enough to be in a low-budget Ghanaian film...

February, 1974...

I walked into the office of Ato Blaze, the celebrated movie producer.

I was so eager to pick up my paycheck, for a lead role that I had spent all of the previous year shooting.

But nothing can describe the boiling, torrential blood that rose to fill up my head, when I saw that Franklin Quist was getting paid three times the amount that my check was worth, for a much less daunting role and he was a much less celebrated actor.

I huffed and puffed about it, but Ato Blaze said nothing;

And the next year, I acted in a film that revealed the
truth about gender discrimination and equal pay.
Oh, I saw it all and I played them
At one point, or another, I was all of these women.
I was told that these women represented all that the
Ghanaian woman was and could ever be.
Every time that I was on set, I would weep, because I
was treated like a prostitute, who had to beg for her
pay.
I wanted to play the role of a president, or a lawyer, or a
successful singer, or a renowned film maker...
But those roles were reserved for better human beings;
human beings who had thick facial hair, deep voices,
private parts that were different from mine.
And I could never be a man, so my fate was sealed.
Tonight, I sit in my hotel room in Takoradi and watch
the waves of the Atlantic Ocean that kiss Ghana's feet.
Fragments of my life before the cameras, float to me
and then away from me, with the ebb and flow of the
monstrous water currents...
Yes,
Tonight is the night that I'll celebrated as a queen of
the screen, for the last time.
Tonight, I'll wiggle into a body-hugging bespoke gown,
just once more.
Tonight, I'll strut down the red carpet of Ghanaian
film, in six-inch heels, and then I won't look back at my
footprints, because that door would be closed, my trail
hidden.
Tonight, I'll smile for the cameras just one last time...

April 1995...

After having lived 25 years of my life in front of
numerous and varied cameras, I finally became the
single mother, the widow, who is slaving to put her
child through school.

For the first time in 25 years, I felt bold, dignified,
empowered.

I felt that I had evolved and, to me, this meant that the
Ghanaian woman had evolved too.

I recall how my face would be swollen every night; I
would have smiled so much and would have cried my
eyes dry, because every other woman on the streets of
Accra would stop me to speak favour upon my life and
to bless me with their prayers...

I had become their heroine. My work on screen had
shown them what they could be, if they wanted to.

June 1996...

I morphed into a struggling young woman, who stood
her ground and refused to accept financial assistance,
in return for sex.

And Ghanaians hated me for it; but they loved me too.
The Ghana Broadcasting Corporation and The Daily
Graphic couldn't get enough of me.

I led female-empowerment campaigns.

I was icon; not a sex symbol, but the true, big deal,
worthy of everyone's respect kind of icon.
worthy of everyone's respect kind of icon.

And oh, I saw it all and I played them all:

- The wealthy Ghanaian market woman, who made

a show at the bank every Friday, by depositing her
hundreds of millions of Cedis.
- The first lady of Ghana, a woman of repute, in her
own right... not because of her husband's status,
but because she was an accomplished barrister and
songwriter.
- The influential woman, whom was invited to an event
at the African Regent Hotel in Accra, Ghana, which was
strictly by invitation.
- The young lady who works in media, is a poet and is
invited to do a poem at the unveiling of the First Lady
of The Republic of Ghana, as a friend the Black Star
International Film Festival, which is run by yet another
powerful, Ghanaian woman!
Tonight, I sit in my hotel room in Takoradi and watch
the waves of the Atlantic Ocean that kiss Ghana's feet.
Fragments of my life before the cameras, float to me
and then away from me, with the ebb and flow of the
monstrous water currents...
And
Tonight is the night that I'll celebrated as a queen of
the screen, for the last time.
Tonight, I'll wiggle into a body-hugging bespoke gown,
just once more.
just once more.
Tonight, I'll strut down the red carpet of Ghanaian
film, in six-inch heels, and then I won't look back at my
footprints, because that door would be closed, my trail
hidden.
Tonight, I'll smile for the cameras one last time...
No more movies,

No more 18-hour road trips,
No more late moonlit nights and early sunlit mornings
spent
Striving to get into character,
Striving to escape,
Striving to rid myself of personal values, beliefs and
preconceptions,
Striving so hard;
To be some other woman,
To become someone else…
And I shall bow out with Grace, with, with poise, with
elegance, with pride, with a strong conviction:
For I have paid my dues to the Ghanaian Film Industry
And through the pain, through the shame, through
the disappointments, the insults, the triumphs, the
laughter, the sleepless nights and the brazen creativity,
I have succeeded in changing the narrative OF and
FOR the Ghanaian woman.

2018

Urban Issues In Accra

ACCRA LOVE-HATE

There's just something about Accra.
Something about the kenkey.
Something about the kelewele.
Something about the waakye.
Something about the jollof.
Something about the tuo zaafi.
Something about the tatale and the kaaklo and the tsofi and the kofi broke man.
Something about the trotros.
Something about the markets and the yam and the spices and the sobolo and the Kingsbite.
Something about the Jamestown Art, about the Osu paintings, about the art in the arrangement of the tomatoes and the kpakpo shito at Mokola and Agbogbloshie.

The Music! The Fashion! The Weddings!
Something about Brazil House and Bible House and Richter House and the blood-stained Light House.
Something about the colonial buildings and memories manifest in Adabraka, Osu, Ridge and Cantonments.
Something about the street hawkers.
Something about the table-top shops and coconut stops.
Something about the potholes that sit on roads like bad acne.
Something about the old, rusty railways aching to tell their own Accra and Ghana stories.
Something about the flooding and the fast-rising high-rises that make the city so concrete, so distant.
Something about the open gutters and the motor-clad zongos.

Something about the Accra children running across the Accra streets in their over-sized school uniforms and gigantic school bags.

Something about the ministries, the National Theatre, OUR independence Arch.

Something about the lovers who walk amidst the khebab smoke and indomie vapour at 9 pm, struggling to find space to move, caressing each other, holding hands and competing with a taxi for the shoulder of the road.

Something about Accra-Dubai.

Something about the floods.

There's just something nasty, offensive, awesome, tasty, disgusting, painful, scary, aromatic, glorious and beautiful about Accra.

Accra we dey. And each day, I wake up hating to love it.

2017

FOOTPRINTS OF HERITAGE

A part of me comes from Kpone-on-sea (Nii Dun We Clan) in the
Greater-Accra Region.
We are the true Ga-Daŋme
Two-tongued people, who spit both Ga and Daŋme.
We love kokonte and crabs, otim and, of course, kpekple!
My grandfather was a renowned patriarch and goldsmith, so many
of our heirlooms are made of pure gold.

We are a people of dancers and singers and poets;
We are lovers of jewellery and unique, quirky, ethnic fashion.
We are traders and farmers, artisans and fisherfolk.
We are pure in heart and spirit and we respect every man, woman
and child.
We are knowledge-bearers, slaves of intellect, we are the royal
guards of ingenuity,
We are hungry hunters, who traverse the land and battle against
waves, in a restless search-war
for anything that would be likely to saturate our minds set our souls
ablaze with depths of en-light-en-ment
for the creator, for the creature and for all time.

We respect tradition, but we know that culture is dynamic.

And we believe that women, with their hefty curves,
feathery lips,
captivating eyes,
distracting hips and thighs and bottoms,
supple breasts;

They are the driving force towards economic success and communal unity.

We believe in the strength and power that our men wield.
We believe in the healing potency of the sand, of the sun, of the air and of the sea
And of love
And of truth
And of virtue
And of creativity
And of nature
And of identity...
Mijɔ Kpone-On-Sea.
And it's a part of my heritage that I have always been honoured to own.

2017

DEATH SONG

Your lips are blue, almost black, and swollen with yellowish cracks carved into them.
Your cheeks are scorched, deflated tennis balls.
Your stomach is puffed up, in sharp, awkward contrast to your bony, mutilated, fragile frame.
Your eyelids are thin and sunken with dark discoloration.
Your nails are a putrid, mucous-y yellow.

I should stop looking at you. I can't look at you anymore. It's too painful. It's disgusting. This isn't you; this CANNOT be you...
Two weeks ago, we strolled, our hands intertwined in a tangled grip, our childish cores prancing through the streets of Accra Central, our stomachs leading the way to Naa Ami's kenkey table-stall.
You spoke of a new crush and I rattled and chattered and gushed and blushed, with Fiifi's name itching to roll off of my tongue, every other second.
And we couldn't smell the freshness of the hot kenkey:
The humongous trenches of gutters gaped at us, their filthy mouths spewing chunks of rotten tomatoes, decomposing plantain peels, black polythene bags and pure water sachets drenched in sticky, gooey brown clots of filth.
These valleys of filth were full of a thick, blackish-brownish, viscous liquid. Flies the size of my palm danced Agbadza, Kpanlogo, Adowa, calling one another to come discover the nasty treasures intelligent human beings had left for them.
And oh, the stench! It hung heavy in the air and clung to my eyes, my nose, my neck, my back, it clenched my ankles, until I began to lose my balance, faltering forward in a nauseated daze...

And I was disgusted. My insides protested. I doubled over, as intense spasms shook my entire body. I threw up my breakfast in rancid lumps of tea bread, butter, jam and omelette.

And the lumps trickled down to join the chunks of rotten tomatoes, decomposing plantain peels, black polythene bags and pure water sachets drenched in sticky, gooey brown clots of filth.

Anytime I opened my burning eyes, the revolting chunks of rotten tomatoes, decomposing plantain peels, black polythene bags and pure water sachets drenched in sticky, gooey brown clots of filth; the thick, blackish-brownish, viscous liquid; the flies the size of my palm;

They all looked me right in the eye, then I'd continue to throw up my breakfast in rancid lumps of tea bread, butter, jam and omelet.

I said the kenkey was a bad idea. I said that we could not buy food from such a place. You said that the kenkey was tasty, that the best local food joints in Accra were all setup beside gutters. You asked me if I knew what the fancy restaurant chefs did to my food, before it landed on my table, all pretty and delicious looking...

We bought the kenkey. But I felt too sour to eat it with you.

Last week you began to throw up your breakfast in rancid lumps of tea bread, butter, jam and omelet.

Your skin became sticky and sweaty.

Your face was twisted in pain.

You would not see a doctor...

Then on Thursday, the ambulance came to the office; you had collapsed.

I sobbed my heart out, by your sick bed, I couldn't bear to look at all the tubes and needles and the nurses buzzing in and out to look at you, to touch you, to refill your drip bag, to tell me that you were gone!

Now...
Your lips are blue, almost black, and swollen with yellowish cracks carved into them.
Your cheeks are scorched, deflated tennis balls.
Your stomach is puffed up, in sharp, awkward contrast to your bony, mutilated, fragile frame.
Your eyelids are thin and sunken with dark discoloration.
Your nails are a putrid, mucous-y yellow.

I should stop looking at you. I can't look at you anymore. It's too painful. It's disgusting. This isn't you; this CANNOT be you...
Now I'm here, mourning a young life wasted. And now, I know that I cannot be protected from the chunks of rotten tomatoes, decomposing plantain peels, black polythene bags and pure water sachets drenched in sticky, gooey brown clots of filth; because they lurk in the open shadows.
And what should have been a beautiful tribute, is a narrative of pain, filth and
Revolting memories.

2015

AYANA IS MEANT TO BE
A BEAUTIFUL FLOWER

A vile, cancerous, grotesque sore eats at the walls of our proud, societal stomach; we bleed, we vomit blood. We are sick...

Ayana's worn feet scrape the dusty-muddy concrete pavements of Makola, of Accra Central.

Ayana's tortured, clumsy sole angers a pavement tile, it spits and quakes and spins on an invisible pivot.

Ayana, the beautiful flower with huge, dough-y eyes yelps, in a tortured, mangled space of frightful familiarity, of fearful futility, of unfettered, unbearable. PAIN!

Then the angry pavement tile gives way and Ayana's emaciated, life-mutilated skeleton dives into that pit of a gutter.

Ayana, the beautiful flower with huge, dough-y eyes yelps, in a tortured, mangled space of frightful familiarity, of fearful futility; of unfettered, unbearable... PAIN:

Ayana propels her broken self back up, back into this BROKEN world...

Ayana slithers along the dusty-muddy concrete pavements of Makola, of Accra Central.

The filthy, bacteria-infested granules of sand claw at Ayana's knees, they eat into her bloody, red, muddy sores.

A woman click-clacks, briskly by and her market basket slaps Ayana's head;

Ayana's bleeding knees fail her;

She falls flat on her stomach; the ghost of her tattered blouse, which her dead mother bought for her ten years ago, cannot prevent the dusty-muddy concrete pavements of Makola, of Accra Central...

Ayana, in an embarrassed frenzy, prostrates herself, burying her beautiful-petalled-face and the lids of her huge, dough-y eyes in a damp, sticky heap of yesterday's market-rubbish that the garbage truck hasn't collected yet.

Ayana surrenders herself to this tortured, mangled space of frightful familiarity, of fearful futility; of unfettered, unbearable. PAIN...!

It's 4.15 pm, now.

The skies threaten to sneeze tonight.

Misty moments are supposed to nourish beautiful flowers and to rejuvenate our gasoline-charged breaths; to hose down the dusty-muddy concrete pavements of Makola, of Accra Central...

Yet, this Ayana can only dread the thought of a soaked piece of cardboard, another night of mal-nourish-ment, or no nourishment at all.

And in the morning, the robotic SUV's, the racy jaguars and the peeling trotros of Makola, of Accra Central, will splash this Ayana, this beautiful flower with huge, dough-y eyes, with new-muddy-water, washing the blood from her bones, in utter oblivion.

2016

AFRICAN MAJESTY

Agoo!
Our blood is stained with centuries of undermined womanhood!

Our faces are but a reflection of a heritage so femininely majestic.
The chest of the African man is emblazoned by the shadows of
the wretched pain that royal Mother Africa endured, just to birth
him and his generation.
The breasts of the African woman are heavy with a milk that is rich
with the taste of
the blatant intellect,
the sheer strength,
the powerful oratory
And the overpoweringly captivating beauty of the African Queens
who ruled the world, for numerous decades.
Before Mother Africa was overpowered by the schemes of the
coloniser,
The African Queen was our economy.
The African Queen was our politician.
The African Queen was our warrior.
The African Queen was our protector.
The African Queen was our breadwinner.
The African Queen was our farmer, our cook, our dressmaker, our
medicine, our healer, our teacher, our royal nation-builder.
The African Queen was our mother…

Agoo!
I am the Royal African Towncrier!
I am the voice of the extraordinary women, who make our African

heritage drip with the thick honey of royalty, of substance and of pure majesty.
Hear me, when I shout at the top of my lungs that:
Our blood is stained with centuries of undermined womanhood!

Our faces are but a reflection of a heritage so femininely majestic.
The chest of the African man is emblazoned by the shadows of the wretched pain that royal Mother Africa endured, just to birth him and his generation.
The breasts of the African woman are heavy with a milk that is rich with the taste of
the blatant intellect,
the sheer strength,
the powerful oratory
And the overpoweringly captivating beauty of the African Queens who ruled the world, for numerous decades.

We are the descendants of a Womanly Empire.
We walk among the ghosts of royal woman-power and royal woman-fire.
We are free, because of the bondage of royal woman-strength.
We eat the fruits of royal woman-labour.
We live on the back of royal woman-excellence.

And because the African Queens once lived,
Because the African Queens once ate and drank of the Earth's soil and of the sea's waters;
Today,
We are AFRICAN MAJESTY.

2019

Connect with The Author Online:

Facebook: Apiorkor
Twitter: @apiorkor
Instagram: @apiorkor
Snapchat: @apiorkor
Email: asashong@gmail.com
Website: https://apiorkor.com